MAINE

Anita Yasuda

LET'S READ

AV²
BY WEIGL™

ADDED VALUE • AUDIO VISUAL

Go to **www.av2books.com**, and enter this book's unique code.

BOOK CODE

Z250248

AV² by Weigl brings you media enhanced books that support active learning.

AV² provides enriched content that supplements and complements this book. Weigl's AV² books strive to create inspired learning and engage young minds in a total learning experience.

Your AV² Media Enhanced books come alive with...

Audio
Listen to sections of the book read aloud.

Video
Watch informative video clips.

Embedded Weblinks
Gain additional information for research.

Try This!
Complete activities and hands-on experiments.

Key Words
Study vocabulary, and complete a matching word activity.

Quizzes
Test your knowledge.

Slide Show
View images and captions, and prepare a presentation.

... and much, much more!

Published by AV² by Weigl
350 5th Avenue, 59th Floor
New York, NY 10118
Website: www.av2books.com   www.weigl.com

Library of Congress Cataloging-in-Publication Data

Yasuda, Anita.
 Maine / Anita Yasuda.
   p. cm. -- (Explore the U.S.A.)
 Includes bibliographical references and index.
 ISBN 978-1-61913-357-0 (hard cover : alk. paper)
 1. Maine--Juvenile literature. I. Title.
 F19.3.Y37 2012
 974.1--dc23
                         2012015075

Printed in the United States of America in North Mankato, Minnesota
1 2 3 4 5 6 7 8 9 16 15 14 13 12

052012
WEP040512

Project Coordinator: Karen Durrie
Art Director: Terry Paulhus

Weigl acknowledges Getty Images as the primary image supplier for this title.

MAINE

Contents

This is Maine.
It is called the Pine Tree State.
There were once many pine
trees in Maine.

This is the shape of Maine. It is in the east part of the United States. Maine borders New Hampshire and Canada.

Where is Maine?

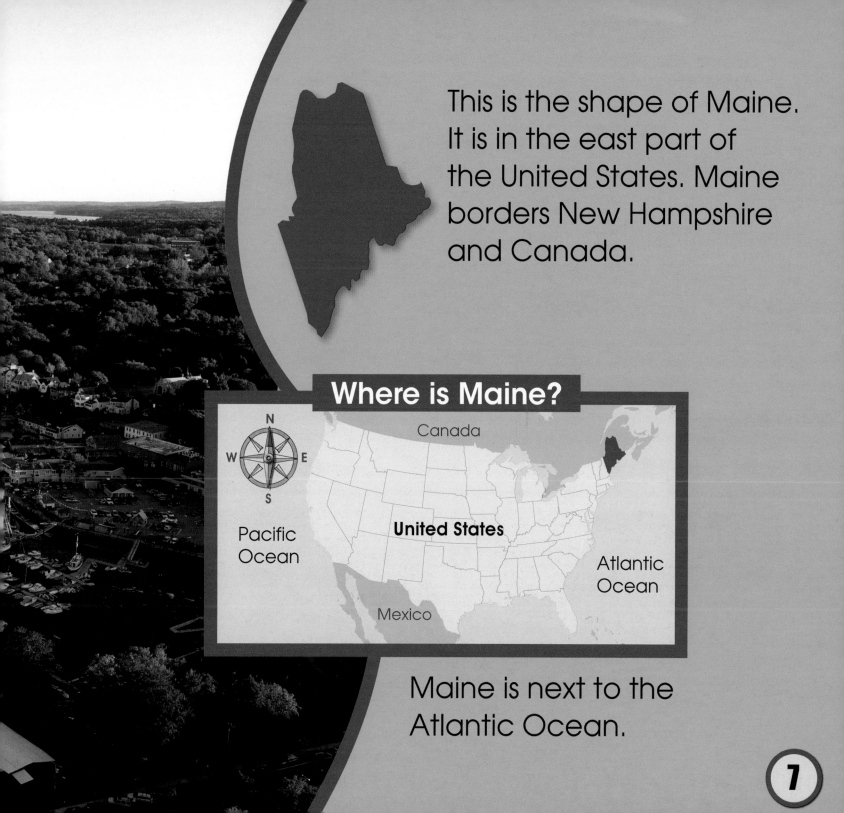

N
W E
S

Canada

Pacific Ocean

United States

Atlantic Ocean

Mexico

Maine is next to the Atlantic Ocean.

Sawmills were built in Maine almost 400 years ago. People from around the world came to work in the sawmills.

One Maine town had more than 300 sawmills.

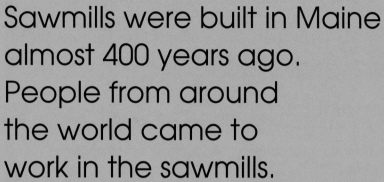

9

The white pine cone and tassel is the Maine state flower. The white pine tree keeps its seeds in these cones.

The Maine state seal has two men, a pine tree, and a moose.

The men on the seal are a farmer and a sailor.

This is the state flag of Maine. It is blue with the same picture as the state seal.

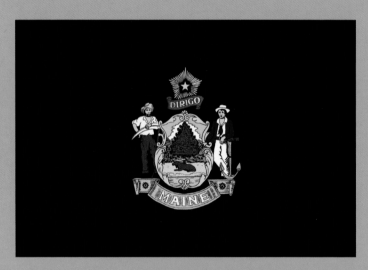

The star at the top of the flag is the North Star.

13

The state animal of Maine is the moose. Moose are the largest member of the deer family. About 30,000 moose live in Maine.

Moose can swim for more than 9 miles.

This is the capital city of Maine. It is named Augusta. The capitol building in Augusta is called the State House.

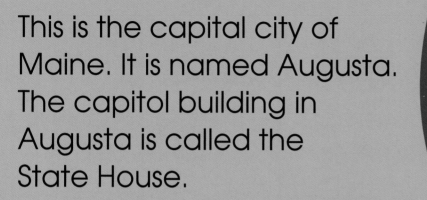

Augusta has the oldest log fort in the United States.

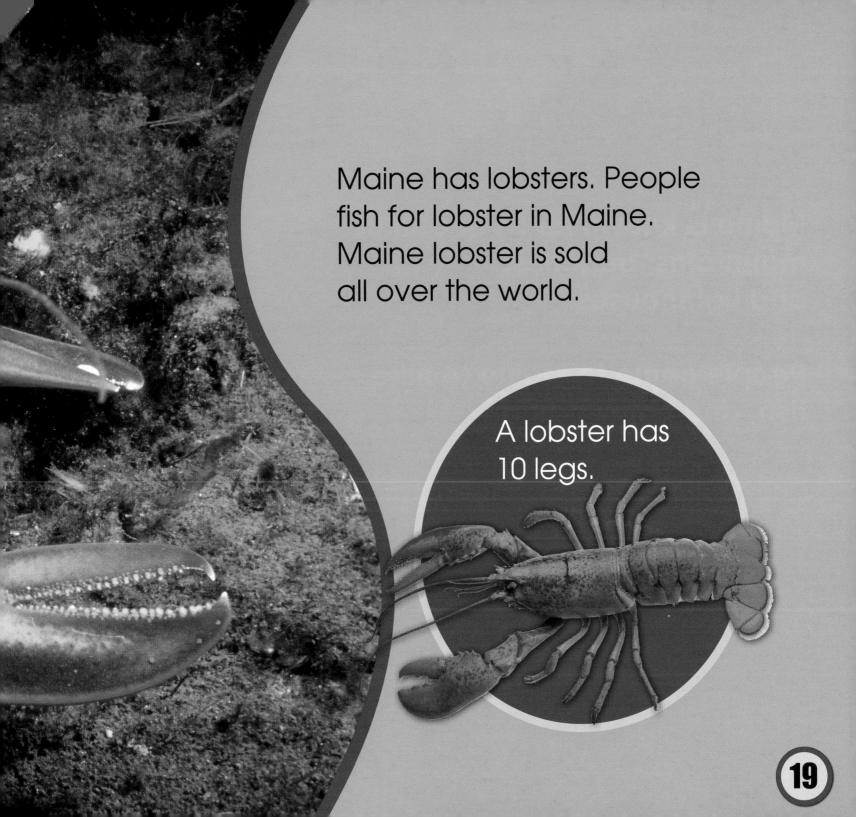

Maine has lobsters. People fish for lobster in Maine. Maine lobster is sold all over the world.

A lobster has 10 legs.

Maine is known for its beautiful
mountains, beaches,
and lighthouses.

People come to Maine to hike,
fish, and enjoy nature.

MAINE FACTS

These pages provide detailed information that expands on the interesting facts found in the book. These pages are intended to be used by adults as a learning support to help young readers round out their knowledge of each state in the *Explore the U.S.A.* series.

Pages 4–5

Maine is nicknamed the Pine Tree State because towering pine trees once dominated Maine's forests. During the 1700s and 1800s, many pine trees were cut down for use in the lumber and shipbuilding industries. Forestry is still an important industry in Maine.

Pages 6–7

On March 15, 1820, Maine became the 23rd state to join the United States. Maine is 33,215 square miles (77,982 sq. kilometers) in area. The state would fit into Texas seven times. Maine borders New Hampshire to the southwest and the Canadian provinces of Quebec and New Brunswick to the north.

Pages 8–9

European explorers came to Maine in the early 1600s. They helped establish industries such as trapping, fishing, and shipbuilding. Mills produced goods such as paper and lumber. Bangor, Maine, once had more than 300 sawmills. It was known as the "Lumber Capital of the World."

Pages 10–11

The white pine cone and tassel became the official state flower in 1895. Maine is the only state whose official flower does not have a flower. The star at the top of the seal is the Polar Star, or North Star. When Maine joined the Union in 1820, it was the northernmost state.

Pages 12–13

The Maine state flag was adopted in 1909. At the top of the flag is the Polar Star with Maine's motto, *Dirigo*, which is Latin for "I Lead." The farmer and the sailor represent the land and sea. Both people are important in Maine's past and present.

Pages 14–15

Maine is one of the few states with a large moose population. Moose can run up to 35 miles (56 km) per hour and are able to dive 18 feet (5.5 meters) or more underwater to find food on the bottom of lakes. Moose are herbivores, meaning they only eat plants.

Pages 16–17

Augusta became the state capital in 1827. Augusta was first an American Indian village. Later, pilgrims set up a trading post near Augusta on the Kennebec River. Augusta's Fort Western was built in 1754. During the American Revolution, the fort was used by Benedict Arnold and his troops to launch an attack on Quebec.

Pages 18–19

Maine is the leading producer of lobster in the United States. More than 104 million pounds (47 million kilograms) of lobster is landed in Maine each year. Maine makes more than $331 million per year from lobster landings. Maine's cold, clear waters and rocky coast make an ideal habitat for lobsters.

Pages 20–21

Visitors come to Maine to enjoy its lakes, mountains, forests, and historic fishing villages. Many kinds of whales are found near the Maine coast, including humpbacks, pilots, minkes, and orcas. People can view whales from shore or take whale-watching tours. Whales are found off the Maine coast from mid-April to October.

KEY WORDS

Research has shown that as much as 65 percent of all written material published in English is made up of 300 words. These 300 words cannot be taught using pictures or learned by sounding them out. They must be recognized by sight. This book contains 57 common sight words to help young readers improve their reading fluency and comprehension. This book also teaches young readers several important content words, such as proper nouns. These words are paired with pictures to aid in learning and improve understanding.

Page	Sight Words First Appearance
4	in, is, it, once, many, state, the, there, this, tree, were
7	and, next, of, part, to, where
8	almost, around, came, from, had, more, one, people, than, work, world, years
11	a, are, has, its, keeps, men, on, these, two, white
12	as, at, picture, same, with
15	about, animal, can, family, for, live, miles
16	city, named
19	all, over
20	come, mountains

Page	Content Words First Appearance
4	Maine
7	Atlantic Ocean, Canada, New Hampshire, shape, United States
8	sawmills, town
11	farmer, flower, moose, pine cone, sailor, seal, seeds, tassel
12	flag, North Star, star, top
15	moose
16	Augusta, building, fort, State House
19	legs, lobsters
20	beaches, lighthouses, nature

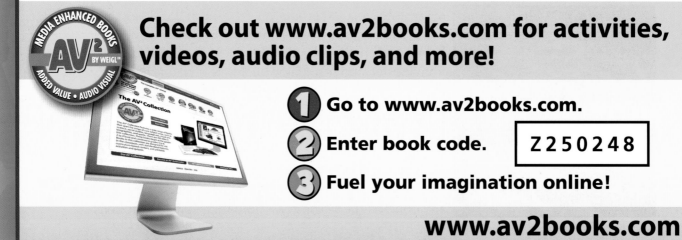

Check out www.av2books.com for activities, videos, audio clips, and more!

1 Go to www.av2books.com.

2 Enter book code. Z250248

3 Fuel your imagination online!

www.av2books.com